Classic MOVIE
INSTRUMENTAL SOLOS

Arranged by Bill Galliford, Ethan Neuburg and Tod Edmondson

Alfred Cares. Contents printed on 100% recycled paper.

© 2010 Alfred Music Publishing Co., Inc.
All Rights Reserved. Printed in USA.

ISBN-10: 0-7390-7006-1
ISBN-13: 978-0-7390-7006-2

Contents

DING-DONG! THE WITCH IS DEAD

(from The Wizard of Oz)

Track 1: Demo

Music by
HAROLD ARLEN

Moderately bright march (♩ = 116)

Ding-Dong! The Witch Is Dead - 5 - 1
35122

CANTINA BAND

(from *Star Wars Episode IV: A New Hope*)

By
JOHN WILLIAMS

Moderately fast ragtime (♩ = 112)

Cantina Band - 4 - 1
35122

17

To Coda ⊕

25

10

CONCERNING HOBBITS
(from *The Lord of the Rings: The Fellowship of the Ring*)

Track 3: Demo

By
HOWARD SHORE

14

JAMES BOND THEME

By
MONTY NORMAN

Track 4: Demo

Moderately bright (♩ = 138)

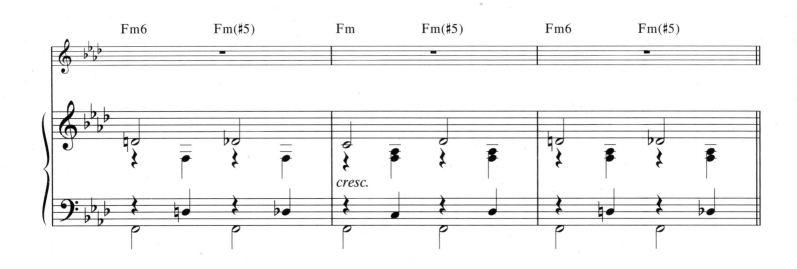

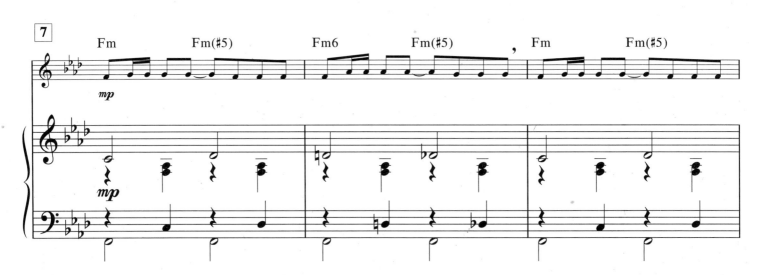

The James Bond Theme - 4 - 1
35122

The James Bond Theme - 4 - 2
35122

18

With a slight swing feeling

Track 5: Demo

GONNA FLY NOW
(Theme from *Rocky*)

By
BILL CONTI, AYN ROBBINS
and CAROL CONNORS

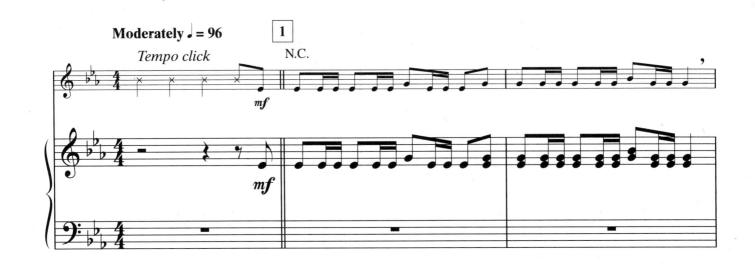

Gonna Fly Now - 4 - 1
35122

22

RAIDERS MARCH

By
JOHN WILLIAMS

Track 6: Demo

Raiders March - 4 - 1
35122

20

Track 7: Demo

FAMILY PORTRAIT
(from *Harry Potter and the Sorcerer's Stone*)

By
JOHN WILLIAMS

Slowly, with expression (♩ = 80)

* An easier 8th-note alternative figure has been provided.

32

HEDWIG'S THEME
(from *Harry Potter and the Sorcerer's Stone*)

By
JOHN WILLIAMS

Misterioso (♩ = 160)

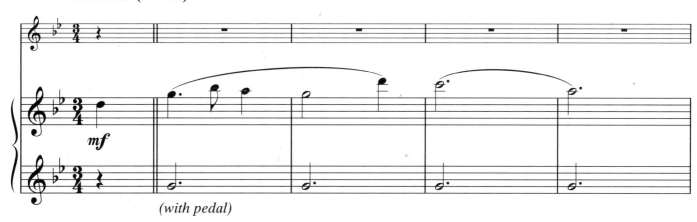

(with pedal)

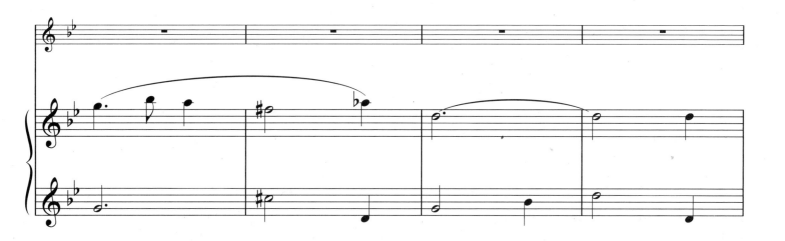

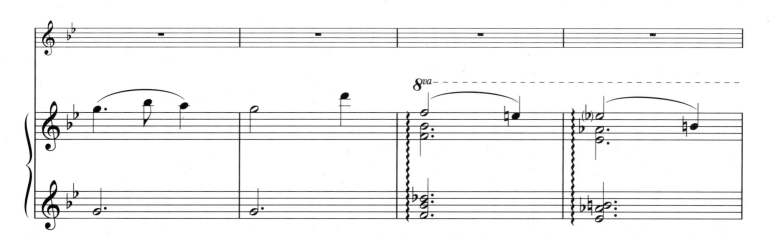

Hedwig's Theme - 5 - 1
35122

STAR WARS
(Main Theme)

Track 9: Demo

By
JOHN WILLIAMS

Majestically, steady march (♩ = 108)

Star Wars - 5 - 1
35122

40

simile

Track 10: Demo

IN DREAMS
(from *The Lord of the Rings: The Fellowship of the Ring*)

Words and Music by
FRAN WALSH and
HOWARD SHORE

Moderately slow (♩ = 76)

(with pedal)

In Dreams - 3 - 1
35122

Track 11: Demo

SONG FROM M*A*S*H*

(Suicide Is Painless)

Words and Music by
MIKE ALTMAN and JOHNNY MANDEL

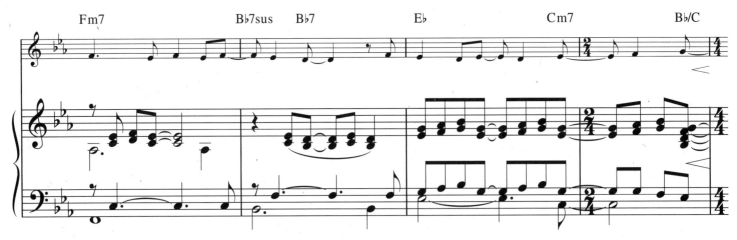

Song from M*A*S*H* - 3 - 1
35122

48

Track 12: Demo

OVER THE RAINBOW

(from *The Wizard of Oz*)

Music by
HAROLD ARLEN

Slowly, with expression (♩ = 88)

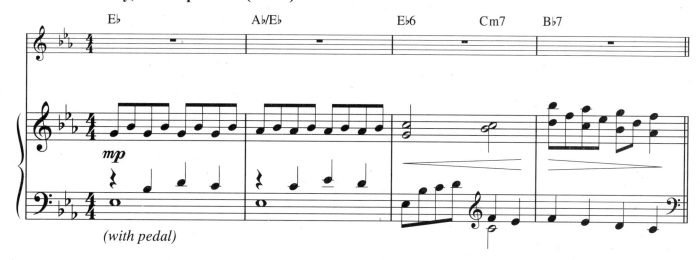

(with pedal)

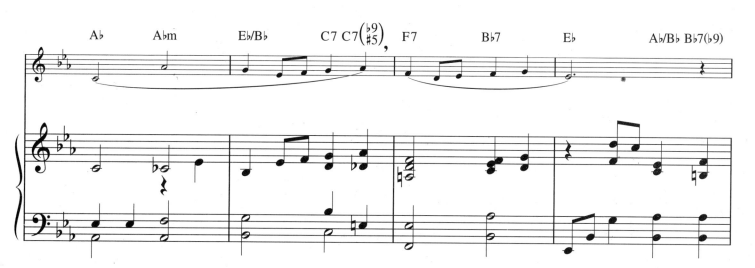

Over the Rainbow - 3 - 1
35122

KEEP YOUR STUDENTS PLAYING WITH THESE GREAT PLAY-ALONGS

Arranged for Flute, Clarinet, Alto Saxophone, Tenor Saxophone, Trumpet, Horn in F, Trombone, Piano Accompaniments, Violin*, Viola* and Cello*.

* Piano Accompaniment included

LEVEL 1

Easy Christmas Instrumental Solos
Book & CD

Easy Popular Movie Instrumental Solos
Book & CD

Easy Rock Instrumental Solos
Book & CD

LEVEL 2–3

Classic Movie Instrumental Solos
Book & CD

Harry Potter™ Instrumental Solos
(Movies 1–5)
Book & CD

Indiana Jones and the Kingdom of the Crystal Skull Instrumental Solos
Book & CD

Lord of the Rings Instrumental Solos
Book & CD

Selections from Rolling Stone Magazine's 500 Greatest Songs of All Time: Instrumental Solos, Volumes 1 and 2
Book & CD

Star Wars® Instrumental Solos
(Movies I–VI)
Book & CD

Top Praise and Worship Instrumental Solos
Book & CD

The Wizard of Oz Instrumental Solos
Book & CD

—— Visit **alfred.com** for more information ——

INSTRUMENTAL ENSEMBLES FOR ALL SERIES

Arr. Michael Story

A versatile, fun series intended for like or mixed instruments to perform in any combination of instruments, regardless of skill level. All books are in score format with each line increasing in difficulty from grade 1 to grade 3–4. Perfect for concerts with family and friends, recitals, auditions, and festivals. Available for brass, woodwinds, strings, and percussion.

Movie Duets for All

Titles: Double Trouble • In Dreams • Singin' in the Rain • The Entertainer • Twistin' the Night Away • We're Off to See the Wizard • Be Our Guest • Fame • Wonka's Welcome Song • Wizard Wheezes • Can You Read My Mind? • Star Wars • Everything I Do • I Don't Want to Miss a Thing • Living in America • Gonna Fly Now • Superman Theme.

Movie Trios for All

Titles: Believe • As Time Goes By • Can't Fight the Moonlight • How the West Was Won (Main Title) • If I Only Had a Brain • Nimbus 2000 • You've Got a Friend in Me • Mamma Mia • Batman Theme • Cantina Band • Imperial March • James Bond Theme • Theme from Ice Castles (Through the Eyes of Love) • You're the One That I Want • Raiders March.

Movie Quartets for All

Titles: Hedwig's Theme • Over the Rainbow • And All That Jazz • The Magnificent Seven • Theme from A Summer Place • Eye of the Tiger • There You'll Be • Blues in the Night • The Pink Panther • You're a Mean One, Mr. Grinch • Parade of Charioteers • Hakuna Matata.

Alfred